Praise for Melanie Siebert

T0205011

"The beauty of the double-head thera[...] [...] through these lightly water-haunted poems, where 'a dipper works the dusky edges/with underwater vision.' The talkers in all the sessions here have such vision and more. The stakes are high. One voice has 'stolen depression as a perfect disguise,' and this is only the starting point for them; another wants to die. *Signal Infinities* is gripping, heart-tearing."
—Tim Lilburn, author of *Numinous Seditions: Interiority and Climate Change*

"A stunning, intricately intelligent book about porousness—the vulnerability of all beings to their environments—as both an axis of harm and a tool of resistance. When 'ungovernable winds lift the patented seeds,' what might it look like to join forces with those winds? Which is to say, let ourselves be carried too. Beautiful, surprising, provocative work." —River Halen, author of *Dream Rooms*

"In other times, mind and world were one and the body was a manifestation of that unity. Today, we suffer separation and therapy is the navigation of contradictions. In *Signal Infinities*, Melanie Siebert returns mind to the world and the world to the body so that 'the polyamorous sea' is coextensive with 'a surplus of irretrievably private coulees.' There is no therapy for truth, no cure. Reading this book, I felt the sublime terror of true poetry. I write this with tears in my eyes." —Matt Rader, author of *Fine*

"In Melanie Siebert's *Signal Infinities*, bodies meeting one another in a therapist's office are sentient bodies of water. Whether our bodies are suicidal, grieving, and dissociating, or assessing, diagnosing and making case notes, a great knowing lake of water is distributed among us and it 'intuits a blown-off-course blue.' These poems trace, in therapeutic encounters, a 'limnology of survival,' of lake reading lake, as the poet gauges another water's struggle to return, through care and relation, to flows of deep self-recognition. I loved this book for convincing me that the water in all of us is one system, striving always for balance."   —Sonnet L'Abbé, author of *Sonnet's Shakespeare*

"Amidst the relentless background static of catastrophe—colonialism, ecocide—Melanie Siebert's finely-tuned poems gather focus. *Signal Infinities*, mutable and kinetic, 'osprey-eye alert,' offers a means to attend to the unknowable otherness of the traumatized world, the body, and memory. The imperative of Siebert's profession becomes a pulsing refrain, 'do no harm / do no harm' but also, crucially, '[d]o something.'"   —Sheri Benning, author of *Field Requiem*

"Melanie Siebert is a poet who wields lines of intense complexity and simplicity, of compression and release, seemingly without effort."
—Philip Kevin Paul, author of *Little Hunger*

SIGNAL INFINITIES

A POEM

MELANIE SIEBERT

McClelland & Stewart

McClelland & Stewart and colophon are registered trademarks of
Penguin Random House Canada Limited.

2 lines from "Practical Water" from *Practical Water* © 2009 by Brenda Hillman.
Published by Wesleyan University Press. Used by permission.

Published simultaneously in the United States of America.

Library and Archives Canada Cataloguing in Publication data
is available upon request.

ISBN: 978-0-7710-1398-0
ebook ISBN: 978-0-7710-1400-0

Cover design by Dylan Browne
Cover images: Christina Mackie
Typeset in FS Brabo by Sean Tai
Printed in Canada

McClelland & Stewart,
a division of Penguin Random House Canada Limited,
a Penguin Random House Company
www.penguinrandomhouse.ca

1 2 3 4 5   28 27 26 25 24

CONTENTS

& there were in the hearts of the water molecules
little branches perpendicular to thought

—BRENDA HILLMAN

SIGNAL
INFINITIES

WATER TAKES UP THE OFFICE

As if breath has sourced a new element,
    a charged conductivity,
      proteins holding open each cell's gates,

water or something like water presses in.

As if a fine mist wicks
        between this thought and the next.

Or a remnant of a great inland sea.

A sheen of gulls,
  a painterly swoop disregarding modernity,
    a feeling like an electric field
          pours into
    a trough dug by glaciers,

    as if a lake parallel to the prevailing winds,
      calls forth
    wind-mixing dynamics,
        a place to sink to.

Or a raindrop's interior.

~

The therapist keeps trying to prove her molecules
are really made of water, that she could flow
with any pitch.

She adores water.
Then forgets to drink.

She adjusts her socks.

Salt makes the cracker she eats.

   (through a window rain splatting the parking lot)

   (distant rocky bluffs porpoising above their colonial names)

   (glacial grooves, a slow buckling)

Or is water itself the therapist?

~

The lake wears no make-up.
A medium without clearcut
theories. Lake's pants crumpled
on the floor all week shake out smooth.

Freud, the therapist thinks, is a school of trout
travailing in a slanting, moody light.
Jung, the fingerlings and their shadows.
More interbeing than they could admit.

The lake develops infrared images of the surrounding
animals ghosting the night's hedges.
A blue-collar wind clocks in.

The lake intuits a blown-off-course blue,
a meringue-peaked
                    then chasming blue.

   Bending light.

Lake is dressed as a tatty but elegant usher,
without a mission except
bare attention.

~

Sometimes this water rises to their knees,
the therapist and the one who wants to die.

Or the one who has tried to die.
Has three attempts and ten diagnoses.

Or the one with a serious pill stash, some graphic poems.

Or thoughts pinballing, logic's ladders flying apart.

Sometimes lake ruffs their shoulders, their necks
 so gently. Like they are stunned
        downed pilots,
     suddenly taking in
        each other, the expanse,
          osprey-eye alert.

Or they are free divers, suspended,
        hair lifting like pondweeds, lungs
            so calmly buoyant
           for as long as the body allows,
             transmuting
        sustenance from what moves
                  through.

     Sometimes.

Lake overflows the
idea of an hour.

THE SESSIONS
ON REPLAY

(refractions, waves bending)

(as if in the present)

(an attempted address)

(therapist to the no-longer-present *you*)

(to the many *yous*)

(living or dead, that isn't necessarily known)

(leaning into lake's reflection)

(two people simply)

(phones on silent)

(even as most creatures on earth have never seen human beings)

Each session begins with a steady voice

With cinematic rules,
with tailfeather light.
Sit wherever you like.

*Lake adheres to the sacred prohibition
against making an accurate image.*

Two bodies uneasy
in their signals,
with thrifted and fast
fashions covering, cutting in, draping
oddly, gaping maybe, rearranging
again and again.

Each wearing our shades of earth,
our gendered angles and metal,
wearing our checkboxes
for normal, average, safe, good enough,
plus some version of crooked teeth,
in-jokes, perpetual spinoffs, crashing
surf, fallen leaves and things
crushed on our treads.

With the ability to wait
and hyper-hearing of an animal in hiding,
wearing our DNA glitter, its private
and glinting beyond.

Open-ended questions seek the revelation of social circumstances and emotional reactions

Within the spired sequence of clinical criteria,
the tight hot spats of rationality,
the canon of white men breathing scientifically
down the neck. I want to be smart.
Normal is a stiff, fashionable suit I've paid for.
I'm not saying they're not useful questions.
They have an adored trajectory in their spearpoint intentions.
They could eat a horse.
Charged glance-for-glance with an observer effect.
Not so good with the memory that bypasses language.
Not so good with the extinguished behaviour of reaching out,
the blizzard snowing inward
or the urge to run.

Clinician asking for your crystalline form

I get it, I take it, I'm an unsafe agent,
trained in a deliberate cadence,
with a bent to formulation.

My body now is meant to signify openness.
There is nothing too guttural, too blasted,
too trackless, nothing that can't be said.

Yes, my scope is trained in a direction.

Too rarely I notice the lake noticing me.

Lake's pitching lamps
undo our practiced faces.

Rigged impossibly

The body wishes nine out of ten to die.
Still wearing chic villain energy
and a monochrome look
with such unbridled oxygen affinity.

Breath arising oiled and improvised
as wind off a cooling mustang's back,
breath lifting like a dragonfly
with its near perfect killrate,
                  slaloming
expertly from the beginning
  the whiteout gates.
                  You
shake a dice etched with the famous suicides.

Still you want to live

      even as a shoe found
        where the creek relents,

      even as a sheet metal hanger, the half-built
        water plant glinting in cursorial light
        with gut pain dark as a pipe draining
        a runaway glacier,

      even as a jackrabbit's rivered ears
        backlit with wildfire
        and so precisely trained.

I SAY THE WRONG THING OVER AND OVER

My voice mimics a fish caught in freeze-up
              thrust months later
                       into air by ice.

Your move, your mind, a changeable instant.

                  Mine 10 seconds at least behind.

Pain that was not knowable as pain arrives.

Our auric circles expand the air.

Simultaneous life plans and death plans
held in a stunning tension.

Flexing with physical ordeals recounted
and recoded as best we can,

even geologies of agony later,
the body doing its shadowy replays.

I guess death is snowfall still riding in the clouds.

WATER LEAKS FROM YOUR EYES, YOU SAY, FOR NO GOOD REASON

As one tear enters the office.
Losing edges and choiring
neurochemical potential.

Lake administers
only nearness.

DMs still light your pocket.
Who cares, you say.
An epigenetic inheritance smuggles a knife grip.

One kitten named Vault bequeathed to an aunt.
Vanishing is explained in a note not yet sent.

You radiate an ultracold cavern
born before stone.
With death a freedom logic.
With a plan to end it, supplies acquired.
With one being no pain and ten being unbearable pain
do you believe in a hereafter?

We accept a black box is sinking in our depths.

Water is willing to be student of the shaking hand.

The hand refusing to be frozen.

THE PAPERWORK IS SHODDY, NO-FLY HEAVY WEATHER
TILTING A DESK

The mouth I don't know how or if it attached to the breast.

The criteria are met or not.

>One wore too many coats.

>One did not want to die badly enough.

>One didn't know how to pick up the phone.

>One didn't know how to put words to it.

>One couldn't take the walls.

Suspensions loopholing what can be said.

You refused.   *Lake reflects.*

You numbed as was necessary.

You stole depression as the perfect disguise.

You feinted hard and fire-blacked the memory.

You black-out-brilliant fled leaving by the only route out.

You internalized the unlivable conditions, but not completely.

You dreamt the sheer opposite, don't forget.

We talk as tassel grass threads the undulations
    housing sky, light energy turning
        to sugars and tiny claws,

the water striders' silky divots, bluegreenblacks
    vaulting our metaphysics
        as a dipper works the dusky edges
            with underwater vision.

You make a covert gesture

Let's say at least once per minute.
A surplus of irretrievably private coulees.

You expand unfixably in the crucial last seconds.

And god that's beautiful
and throws me.

I walk you out

The door closes and I have a sandwich, notes to write
and a face I don't recognize.

At once surviving by hiding.

At once a leafless branch describing the atmosphere.

Eyewells prickling with a craving to be held.

Glorified disorderly by sunshine.

Subject to water.

*Lake admits anyone
with a blue score.*

Ice moves like a lynx swimming.
Disappearing skinny and bedraggled on a far shore.
Renouncing our momentary eye-lock.
Everything strange with pain
and not naming pain.

METABOLIC AND MINERAL

(hour by hour)

(fluctuating)

(sessions cont'd)

(the galaxies we can't see outnumber the ones we can)

Somatic psalms

This hour the body stutters above cliffs.
The body chambers an unspecified charge.
It wants real effing money.
Bones and teeth conduct vibration and temperature.
The body knows how to use the natural threat of size.
It rat-a-tats a scalded jump,
then woah woah woah
    an embryonic flexion response
        to curl into a starless snowstorm.

~

I sit specific
  and local

      someone swallowing half their few words
      someone gathering crooked child feelings
        with the feeble curses of a boxed ear
       with the intent to cancel unnecessary subscriptions
       with stains I've blotted furiously
        with the phantom pain of another life

  practicing

something like opening.

~

This hour the body wears a smashed-
bathroom-door smile, then the blurred
brushstrokes of a glacial retreat, then sideward
and without involvement of the eyes
an inflicting smile, a poisoning-dogs smile
then idling the failing-and-harmless smile
slight hints of eye-muscles reserved
for the mother's approach morphologically
resembling unfurling smoke.

~

This work involves an automatically locking door,
a key forming the interior of one hand
and not the other,
the protocol of elsewhere.

Elsewhere being a pamphlet in a strong breeze,
the map's pinhead pixelating into an anthill,
a cold florescence of plastic chairs,
no place to uncompose.

Refusing to send desperate people elsewhere,
then making my own cortisol from the ether.

Thieves' names flap from the mountains
that cradle the office nevertheless.
Mortality, a limit we all abide.

~

This hour the body's going broke like a stony plain

    without language
        just the faintest grass wind

collecting loosed debris of a stepmother's head injury,
father still smash-mouthed in his trailer,

skiff being taken on the rocks.

~

This hour not crying not giving never
rivering the body all night
an empty convenience store
where no bells no alarms
go off, no one appears.
Smells like dust, shelves of
dust untouched.

~

We are searching
for a story with internal coherence,
one that can meet
the shambled particulars
and the muscle memory
with limber bonds,
                something
where the feet still know
 exactly how
          to balance lightening
       shoes
  on the edge
of a wall
    of flowers.

~

The body drifts into emerg like a pile of leaves
only to be swept back out.
If the chain-linked past has got a stink on you, got you
word salad like pearls spraying from a chokehold,
got you swiveling sheer alienation,
got you a hard blot nothing,
a record,
or just please please trying
to vanish into a wall
+++ racialized, colonized, dumped on.
Then what?

~

Your name is on a waitlist
but that's about as good as scrawled
inside a pizza box a seagull stands on.

I can't forgive a paper with a few phone numbers
given to someone too scared to use a phone.

I can't forgive the door to the street.

It's been shown a fly that's a voracious eater
could coax gardens on Mars.
The soldier larvae will be dedicated
to the outer-space lettuce cause.

~

Then one stops showing.

>   Maybe you're skyhooking a basket

>   or ghosting with sideslip hips
>   a crushing pressure

>   or

>   I don't know.

~

Parliament has declared another crisis.
Apps are deployed as if
they were bees lifting
a flower's DNA.

The coroner's report wins the prize
for most gutting poem
                              but who
     makes it to the end.

Empathy is a sad little gutter.
Reports flop like salmon stranded in a field.
I'm trying to weave in the atmospheric rivers
but maybe that's too much.

~

Sleeplessly sound is bending through
elemental balconies. My night
soundtrack seemingly ripped off

has the feel of someone else's in-patient looping,
wavering
     traffic-edged, wanting
        the phosphorescing dive in.

~

You're a fine needle registering
      to the best of your ability
  the pulses, the calvings,
        the unlivable
    power dynamic pressing your throat.

      Unforgivably I'm asking
  you to live it, live with it
      a little bit longer even
    when we have no balm
      or credible fix.

~

The reason for living could be
to find a reason for living.

The body wants a small gold
cross on a sunning chest.

Pronouncing *sun* perhaps
    we are trekking
      toward each other
        from a great distance.

~

Still simultaneous life plans and death plans.
So we pay reverence to the multiple pulls,

to the confusing asymmetry
between what you know and what you feel.

Sensations surfing from the trigger zone.
The body flushes and regenerates

with its capillary helplessness.
It harnesses an impervious gaze

as necessary. A flux
silted with rarity. The differentials

swishing in our currents, as exhaustion
finds a wolf-bed in me.

~

This hour the body admitted,
     bristling with a locked-door buzz,
          cheeking meds,
     cursing the open-back gown,
   exhausted like moth versus glass.

No regrets, except left on *Read* by a crush.
Not expecting anyone to make it in.
Words unforming in the empty fridge years,
sucked into stone's infancy.
Eats applesauce only, hates daylight.

Until selectively, so selectively,
even as cold sinks into the deepest rift,
with a half-squint and an emperor's chest,
you offer a test, going
into blacklisted detail.

~

Judged too wanting too icy too easy
        too detached too get-off-me
    too who-cares too
        high-speed-acrobatics-in-the-nectar-park
nonetheless the body employs the brilliant technology of the needle
    fashioning precisely:
                yes-yes-now—
                        no-not-ever—
the dignity of choice
    and the careening ride
beyond good and bad, the feathery
    spruce-whorled ground
        readying a bed.

~

Each hour near the stolen diamond
looming like an armed standoff

but the size of a ruffed grouse egg
resting on the distant lake of auctioneer's velvet

tethered invisibly
to 200,000 cubic meters of demolition waste

fibrillating steel and powerlines in the landfill
arson running under the moss

freeze/thaw straining all angles
what heat there is blowing through the gaps

thanks-for-nothing-Canada contaminated
water running over and through

the body always
needing water.

Lake takes in also
without angels
the effluents,
the aircraft tires,
estranged weathers,
and blunted feelings.

~

Together we alter volume and charge,
  forgetting receipts,
    obsolete job descriptions,
      awareness of our own faces.

But not the soft-drink-tacky pavement, the heat
  miraging our most hurt citizens.

Not the wellness checks gone bad,

not the body's hydrologically linked caves,
  the jamming signals, the shifty tolerance,
    our companions in erosion,

not forgetting that sound is touch,

nor the desert horses who can dig
  a well so deep they disappear.

~

To the one who disappears:

      I hope the lack of tracks means you're walking in water.

~

Got to run, got to find the sun-up boat
which the young have paid for earnestly
        amid a death wish.
Here is an interminable crossing,
a case to be argued offshore
before the Supreme Court
of the arctic tern,
black crown and nape,
seeing more daylight than any other,
winding it in
        as pure prowess,
a roguish course,
    owning the tailwinds,
                swooping carnivorous
with the five-speared clarity
    of lightening.

~

Okay glassy and pacing with canyon laughter.

    Okay dilated, irritable, sleeping at odds, nevering the body's legit needs.

        Okay slushy to light, sweaty, hailing a cosmos.

            Okay.

                Okay.

Ice with its clandestine hearing performs
the failure to perform.

TRYING TO READ LAKE'S CASE NOTES

(documenting a mirror feeling)

(distorted in some way)

(these are not the *Iliad*'s soldiers)

(though they are young in their fury)

(their increased ability to register sugar)

(the gods are absent)

(everything happens within the disappearance of ice)

(which is another colonial condition)

(who lives or not, yet unknown)

. . .

[   ]

       biting his hoodie strings
     fountaining Basquiat dreads
     saintly for math's sake
       Gen Z levels of sleep deprivation
his voice is musical code
    his concentration finessed
               to a nanospear
tuned to every test like enemy footsteps

      he has a tight list
         of failings
       doom rides in on

perfection is the elusive protection racket
     running his father's
       stockbroker fever

         he slashes at the list

         has had
            a road trip in mind

     has
       a road trip in mind

As pollen beds down in ice cores and sea floor sediment
and will not be crushed, will not dissolve.

[   ]

play-by-play
future deaths running her mind reel
blotting out TikTok and the posh flim-flam spring
I'm okay I'm okay she says
suicidal a word she won't say
or *death* and anything bad-bad
or even just bad
she's forgiving the peppered moth
industrializing its wings to coal
forgiving the catastrophizing
sunset the flashback
lit at the mere
impulse to speak
forgiving dirty air
the sky's steel vice
the indiscernible triggers
shame invisibly
emanating from the selfies
the boyfriend who pressed his
pain into her pain
the boozy roaming alone
fuck that and sad-song repeats
nights minus the stars except
one back-pocket blade
just in case
she's forgiving the wildfire not yet
deprived of its fuel

As the little brown bats, light-shunning
    vespers dipping their heartbeats to rarity,
      hibernate mostly alone now.

[   ]

their wolf-cut mullet
with a crocus glow at dawn
    nonbinary
grunge meets glam
        from all angles
    owing no one
            any answer

    they punish
fakery with a cruel run

            tornado
    keys
                        into drywall

        been told
every want is too much
        they famine daily
        a version

        of the hated
            self every sharp

                    edge
        counted
            daily

        pain is a way
                not to die

As a measurable electrical field
    naturally occurs during wound healing.

[   ]

her kicks fluid and deadly
running the field
on a half-pack of food bank spaghetti
she scores with both feet
a dangerous
playmaker
at parties
escape plan
weighted in the tide
like fresh-cut hemlock
glistening fat with herring eggs

giving only
moutainface when sober
there's just no way she could say
who

was hurting
her
most nights
her
hummingbird spirit
in a huckleberry jacket
wishes she could still carry
her baby brother

As steadfastly the dusty roadside ferns cool the hidden soil
and intercept rain the road rejects.

[   ]

son of a
logger and a camp cook
born amid
flying pans
amid boom-bust
a company town rotting
in the rain amid
five million tons of slash burning
yearly amid the hush-hush
deaths no one calls suicides

head slammed
once against the newly painted cupboards
once into the front hall's *Last Supper*
once the bathroom sink
once by a friend last seen curled
into the hood dent

he's sobbing
now like his child body never could
before Xanax or whatever curtains back in
slushing again the child need
and the urge to kill
and be killed every night

As a superbly camouflaged dusky whoosh tips
    into its call, into any listener's body.

[   ]

in muddy pixie boots
    her hands paint-splattered
        she's serious
    and unreconciled

                like she's blowing down
        a midnight small-town strip
    something like a fox
        ziplining from the outskirts
            to a dumpster and back

words elusive as
    sibling photos
            never seen
        but existing
                in the files
        of the goddamn
        government

    DJ with the tendency
        of water to flow along
            self-determined pathways
                sampling the sounds
                    of scissors on hair
                spoon stirring a bowl of soup
            the smoothing rasp
                of the swing set
                    where she kindles
                        into a silky comet

                                a channel

As sailing (some jellyfish)

   kiting (some spiders)

      rolling (some beetles)

         blown (some winged things)

            gliding (some at a reduced rate of falling)

[   ]

       pretty is a source
   of comfort   source
      of terror   her unsoothable
            attraction

  the next and the next and the next
          some
      with hands that go
      peaceful or dormant
    some with suddenly flooding fists never
            again fists
       humming easy death fists
         curing you fists feeling
        nothing fists

        ruined and ruining
         fists

    oh she's got her own
     hidden holy fists

    her humiliation-blooming-glory
      fists don't think
      she doesn't   her bestowing
        mercy fists

As an arctic lake begins to hiss, venting
methane, a real unwearable dress.

[   ]

they enter school alone
with the elaborate camo
they've prepped since five a.m.
no eye contact
flat affect
and a matte red statement lip
                    friendlessness a good defense
but each book slam   each chair scrape
is a thorned jolt
each glance of a teacher or classmate
a tyrannical diss
each school day
a chokehold
they evade by cherishing
a secret history
of biological and chemical warfare
mentally stockpiling
tasteless clear liquid

with untold genders they're fleeing
lung muscle
paralysis fountains imagistically
into each passing jogger
                    death visited
with a refined technique
on random
enemies
the necessary
escape

As since the mountaintop has been dismantled
bighorn sheep stutter on air's ladders.

[   ]

lordly
       with boxing
   feints
    hood
always on   face always shadowed
  his guarded body
snapped once   in a vulnerable arrangement
now virally glowing worldwide

  known truly only by razors
    the hot ticket between
      the body's fogged-in coasts
    and the stunner
atmosphere above where sunlight
  rolodexes star power
    where consciousness
     stings brilliant
      and slices alive

As lifted in a sling the last
    Gray Ghost caribou twirls blindly in the air,

      the snowy forest crosshatched
        into sharp shards.

As someone is picking lichen
    to hang from the trees in the pen.

[   ]

the first-time knife held
        to his own throat
      does not emit
absorb or reflect light
in the spring-loaded slapdown
        of five psych reports
ten years later more is unknown
        than known
he's parked at the astronomical twilight docks
        eating hamburgers in a van
            otters hijinxing around   staking territory
        phone rings   isn't answered
                    wet sock smell
      no one worth
talking to   war wounds into war wounds
    into this immigrated wound without war
        teenage in pay rate and sugar love only
          the DUI   dumb fights
        leaving without a look back
            a long practice
        at being crueler than anyone else
            but only to himself
              loathing hauls up
          its silent massive wings
        the body a bruised and scenic
          pressure descending
            without shivers
          a material alteration
                    below observation

As deer saliva talks
    to the cut leaf edge.

[   ]

admitted
she floats
a hard-heeled
loose-armed
strut
sets off
cuss flares
an abyss stare
a carbonizing stare
for the lifespan of a bowhead
she's surrendering only
ash
that's the story   just ash
ash surrendering in an updraft
secretly keeping ███████

one day she may ask for
can't right now
she may ask for
ask for
ask for someone

someone to

or not

she'll ask for whatever
she'll ask for
her bird will be her bird
even the bird
concealed expertly

As tears when falling iridesce
   the chemical make-up of distress, glossy and given

               to air, rising

   with a little warmth off skin.

[   ]

    born programmed for loyalty
   child of dragging
     silence knowing cold
  granite at the center
     bubble wrap on the windows
   blocking out the spitting light
she blames herself for the empties
  the slipups
   leaking intel
  bringing the dreaded knocks
 so her room is a helmet pinning her dizzy head
  blanket heap turning
at the pace of mold
  uneyed she's
  endurance
    born
on the banks of no river
  parched
 valley funnelling
  unseen squalls
    in the nervous
system with
  the weight and reverb of a mother's
    body

   hitting
    the ground

As the whale who would sing for 24 hours straight,
  now without its eerie buoyant violins,

    trails a cinching lead line.

An ocean or so away another whale
  travels back in time

    to decipher the song.

[   ]

sure of her stats sure

of her exception

to the rule sure of her

swimming lats sure

of her sky volume   its windchime

of valid
ID

As the polyamorous sea flings bouquets
  sky high to the continent's brooding edge,

as at least seven empires have fallen
  in the carbon of the disappearing trees.

[   ]

doubting every last feeling
     makes it so hard to live

   combat eyeshadow
      tears rolling the only camera

               her hand cools into Athena's hand
   gripping a kitchen knife

      demanding

      never again never

then a greenroom of insecurities
      cut
   with homicidal flares no doubt
   sensation spin drifting
         fetally
         evoking a blossom

         and the mouth
                  wants nothing
         because there is no way
            to pay

               or just wants

                  nothing

As dolphins spend a morning adorning themselves
with leaves and water's pressure.

[   ]

okay will give
a blow job for being held

that's something

slight and almost lifting

couch surfing   polite for food
and a family vibe like lamplight
wants a mother's
resurrection
after every OD

and a bedroom
just
a bedroom
where the body can be
ordinary
in its animal curl

As without roots, without stems, without a protective film,
    mosses drink water straight from the air,

tendrilling the canopy with the most private swimming pools
    for wheel animals and water bears.

[   ]

a wild rose tattooed at his throat pit
a butterfly for each grandparent
rests on his eat-or-be-eaten
wake wake wake chest
present danger ever
present spiking
without story
strafing
trashed at the center
going through bombed-out motions
jaw locked till
BAM
so jobless
so banned
so nowhere to go
so hazy is a goodness
supplied by a wolf in white socks and slides
and I'm scared you know I'm scared
jumpiness
tamped into the iliopsoas
tightening into a c-clamp
another shot
animal getting away
underbrush full of static
not words but harsh whispers   hatched
baby-spider gods
sometimes sheer hours blooming
music from the body's
one good move

As satellite imagery substitutes for a feeling now,
  cutblocking utmost green

    to cubic gray-green

      to gray asunder.

[   ]

ferocious pendulum of heavy hair
sprinting from the hospital
blonde clock set beating by gravity
insults and desire for a fatal blow
now she's somewhere in the switchgrass
engineered to break down explosives
at the end of running

a police escort to the blue-green
emerg blurs
danger to self or others
no no no she says *I was going somewhere*

two inches to the right, a second
self, motionless
archer merging with the bull's
eye without
a premeditated answer
in the quiet
room where the body is
to be quiet when nothing is quiet
whose bloodwork
comes back the unmeasured   measured
who inhabits the aimless hours
a name tagged neatly
around an unnameable
wrist
the body's dog, she decides,
is already in heaven
flushing prey
for her sustenance

As wherever there was forest it was holy,
     so said Pacheedaht Elder Bill Jones,

and the insomniac kid floundering in cargos,
     and the murrelet flying through water,

scoring a single sandlance
     then weaving a boggling route through

the forests' fog-robed maximalists
     and baroque candelabras

to its solitary hidden chick.

[   ]

acne-scarred steep
angled cheeks
lacrosse abs and calves
a weedy lean
great at cutting   sick fakes   stick work
after-school mover considering the demands
of gravity on a belt
of this or that material
somewhere he's rich in muskeg and geese
and gas drum stoves
shoptalk rising from the eskers
knowing how to use the cold
to advantage
raised on boiled or bottled water
Indian Act water
still spiritual
water
by unalienable rights
he's rich in jerry cans a new outboard
routes through the tricky channels

something's
barely whispered

noctilucent wisps
grazing atmosphere's limit

no he won't go

As the trees
   do not recognize the Crown.

[   ]

she dunks her head in the civil fountain

wet hair redraws

a territory of fitful rivers

city pressed against her shut mouth

city lounging glossy with a fat tab

in her rough, flashing wake

As . . .

Eris	Zoe	Paolo	Carrie	Indi
Frankie	Anita	Bart	Lauren	Dakota
Deanna	Teairra	Gabriel	Lily	Anna
Pablo	Alissa	Leah	Flora	Don
Emily	Scott	Lynne	Natalie	Helen
Inuusaaq	Lindsey	Lex	Megan	Autumn
Rose	Grace	Jennifer	Innosar	Andrea
Cecilia	Benji	Kae	Geraldine	Rosie
Misha	Natasha	Shayda	Natanai	Trina
Ashley	Michael	Jen	Danny	Damen
Kelechi	Guy	Beverly	Teddy	Tarzan
Dior	Sarah	Liz	Nadia	Taboo
Devin	Chantal	Heidi	Corey	Becky
Rochelle	Dominick	Eyvette	Tanaya	Erika
Josh	Sandra	Cayla	Joshua	Mike
Cara	Stephen	Ann	Irene	Isadore
Cei	Shelby	Sabrina	Lorne	Kylee
Jess	Christiane	Melody	Art	Austin
Keris	Mashuq	Nathan	Shane	Jordin
Mindy	Lyndee	Jonathan	Lucy	Tyler
Saranique	Davey	Dorri	Marayne	Rudy
Andy	Brock	Krista	Will	Kisha
Nicolle	Rebecca	Patty	Kaydia	Star
Lagemas	Niomi	Rhett	Zane	Travis
Tina	Zack	Jack	Angela	Halima
Eric	Carlton	Dustin	Kawennáhere	Mike
Logan	Nora	Ken	Joseph	Rhett
Cleo	DeQuincy	Cecelia	Meaghen	Terry
Brenda	Holly	Amanda	Michele	Jordan
Caitlin	Tunchai	Suzanne	Annie	Leah
Marie	Chris	Francesco	Cameron	Grace
Theland	Abel	Kevin	Keaden	Noelle
Kelley	Craig	Kim	Justin	Kat
Matt	Rayna	Peter	Rosabie	Keris
Erin	Meredith	Vyronika	Chasity	Julia
Paul	Rylan	Stacy	Rhoda	Olivia

CONFESSIONS
TO A LAKE

(as a water body emerges)

(in the assembly of my I)

(the therapist with her therapist)

(like dippers genuflecting on rocks and logs)

(with the multiplying presences)

(the actual lakes fed by ice for only a few wars longer)

(so many signals off the charts)

Eventually I acknowledge I can't really remember my childhood

It's a staticky channel, a grip going numb
as equinoxes slide moods into more and less
severe angles.

Until something internal flutter-kicks
like aspen, secretive, wordless,
twisting in the slightest wind.

The blood of Christ trembles in
the tray of clinking sip-sized glasses
    passed over my head,
the chill of grape juice already tasted
on the sly in the church basement.

Kids trickle down the road to school.
Air Jordans kicking gravel,
        coveted like cable TV.
            Bare legs in winter, so cool
in a not-yet-raptured town without a bank or bar.

It was a sad little parade
but I'm not sure I knew that yet.

The caragana shelterbelts required no care
and caught soil trying to leave.

~

The sermon was surgery performed
directly on my open chest, the pastor's
chin dipping almost into hell.

Our fathers bowed like pumpjacks
with the underappreciated grace of donkeys.

Original thoughts stalled
like jars of pickles in the cold room.

We were straight pins in our mother's mouths.
No was a feeling we didn't have words for.

All the kids had bobbed in the HELP position
and felt what a thin layer of water the body warmed.

~

I was not a good person.

The river was my good person
forgiving my unforgiven
   again and again,
      goldsmithing
  light bashing the pebbled
    bottom, then bottomless
        emerald, then black.

~

One born with sin.
One scrubbed and scrubbed.
One hollering.
One already touching oneself.
One already ugly.
One incessant with need.
Disavowed collapsing dust and gas,
in the seventh week of crying
such diaphragmatic force forming.

~

I'm pretty sure at one time
no was a funnel cloud battering the ribs.

Or an electric charge on skin
I didn't know was my own.

But eternity was more insistent,
the sound of a ringing nail pounded
through the church sound system.

We traipsed to flight school,
visible air in the heels, ball shorts,
with jackets open to snow.
Chicago Stadium was a distant planet
the size of a chunky TV,

Jordan highflying zeal
into our possibilities.

We were physical and alive in the gusts,
the scrimmages and wind sprints, eating
two-cowboy lunches in a ruckus,
grazing hands when slipping notes.

But we learned to renounce our bodies.

In so many ways and rooms
it's hard to say.

~

I don't know how many were in the cold parade,
spaced out to what degree.

In spring, the bear who had raided our freezer loped
away, guts unravelling, hooking on the undergrowth.

Ketchup tins and milk cartons protected the seedlings,
yellow poly rope hung the swing.

There I dragged my hair in the grass,
needing that upside
         down,
    my feet in the sky's
      far-flung fissures.

The aspen kept the solution to cleaning guns
and removing nine-tenths of human scent.

The shot bear unseen, ahead, radiating heat even now
in my cagey sleep, my restless-leg corpse pose,
still brushing my childhood
along the tangled, barely discernible
trail, the bear's wet leaves.

~

Did nurses pick up the baby whose mother had been
sent home when the baby wouldn't eat?

The baby surely a squall that would run out of energy.
The hospital named after a thin-lipped queen.

We could have named it after the fescue grasses
called up in rain shadow, or after the parent material

of soil laid down in the last glacial advance,
where most ignition sources were human not lightning.

But the baby was not born into a time
immemorial relationship with the grass.

The baby already had a starvation bent, a shutdown
knack, white clenched fists that could become

missionary fervor, if they believed
in their own defectiveness truly enough.

The grasses untied their long tresses in private.
They were not called to be nurses.

Sure enough sinfulness entered
on the seventh night of squalling.

The steel plow had been invented.

~

I'm of the hungry people denying hunger.   *Hwunitum*
The white foam people moved by wind.   *Yonega*
Takers of the fat.   *Wasicu*

The Indian Act's rich taste on our fingers.
Imperial Metals et al. implored
the death of a star. We learned
a language that poured authority
like cement over the plants' ears.
As wolves maximized the cut lines,
caribou robbed our sleep only a little.

We can say we've studied the deformities,
the weakening skin and mouthparts,
how jets scramble the frogs' synchronicity,
the new fire regime,
chum swimming among picnic tables.

Guilt has the tranquilized
heft of a bear trying to wake up.

Elder Bill Jones hypothesizes
grief in the Premier's heart
as the ancient trees keep falling.

My body has its dead zones.

~

Each year rocks float to the surface of the plowed field.
Imagine the frostbitten dictator, a hungry
boy in loose pants, beaten, a clear tenor,
a rangy teen studying to be a priest,
with talents in poetry and robbery.

No theory explains all the dust in the universe.
The choice to stay or flee.

To cross the border, one hid an abscess in her side
with her child held close.

One prayed doves would carry potato peels
so there would be soup.

One remembered the plums, the fried robin's egg.

One was forced to dig up his father's grave
to prove they had no guns.
Every shovel became that shovel.

One folded a paper boat.
It could be flattened and reshaped
into a boat.

~

What force it took to pull the stumps from the land.
Each lung remained a suitcase packed.
Hazardous spills bloomed in our hands.
We asked plants to evolve a salt tolerance.
We asked potatoes not to blight, not to bruise.

Yet the ungovernable winds lift the patented seeds.
Like when the congregation sang,
      my lungs, ribcage, field of vision, everything
          expanding with the waves.

~

Hail made us as real as the trampled crops.
Slugs did not say their sorries to the greens.
Our freezers shuddered in their duty to meat.

We all knew loneliness more so than hunger
could be a blade or a mirror or merely a stone
worked hard as any chore, unyielding.

A baby could be set adrift in a basket.
As proof our mute organs sailed bravely
through the dusky reeds.

~

Just a boy, scorched in the fields, my father
lifted the coldest living water from the well.

The barn cats shoaled my young mother's warmth
and made their wishes known so freely.

I was an unworldly fresh start
unthinkingly reclaiming the dirt.
A man and a woman had become
a bird flying out of my mouth.

They wanted to give what they didn't have.
They scraped the meat from the bone.
Their sweat combusted into corn.
Music had a strict measure, undone.

My new ten-speed blazed like pure oxygen.
I learned pleasure in a shirt with a gold pinstripe

as the chokecherries crescendoed
toward a brazen equality, almost
marrying me to the earth.

That was before and after a prophet
reached in and pulled out my burning city.

We hiked into the postcard mountains,
knelt to drink right from the streams.
The mountains were allowed
to flaunt their finery.

Our lungs were working
free of their stone tablets.

~

So often I don't know how I feel.

Cirrus feathers icy cirrus,
        producing fall streaks,
            wind shear
            rhythming barely a here.

Then a common cloud progression
to featureless rain.

I confess my hand smells good.

Pollen dusts the unmarked graves
and the thief's cuffs.

It survives being fired from a gun.

~

Some memories are only dizziness,
a choking sensation, words don't surface.
Numbness asks for attention.

Too early the hills are scrawled
with dry grasses ready to burn.

The burdened sky works
on my vanishing point.

Land-sky perfusion discloses a color
as hard to describe as pain,

                a pain with
the capacity to befriend ice and its slow rollercoasters.
It gives instructions to touch my injured leg.

Love is not necessary just touch.
Start there.

A maneuver flown
for motion-generating reasons,
nerves inspiriting like grass
flickering hieroglyphically
from beyond the limit
of the sunlit zone.

Lowest recesses in flow.
Sensation.

Not saved, not denied,
not fire, not a dove.

Giving way to the living,
holy-unholy sluice.

That's all.

Ice slips away.
Without a fuss, without formalities.
Lost self with a powdery heartrate
dropped to 10 beats per minute
and keeping a secret
to the death.

MOTION
JUST BEYOND

(as salmonberry in a green spit-shined phase)

(dialing in the charged sky)

(the body doesn't need to be forgiven)

(for being a body)

Instruments detect a hum

Dark patches appear in the imagery.

Pixels fly up like the Furies flinging
night telekinetically from their tossed locks.

The ice analyst refreshes the screen over and over.

Until the dark shape is open water.

At the place where ice never melts, we register
so partially the breakup of the last shelf.

With immodestly sheer bodies, krill
ear the interior of the crash.

Sleep is far out and sliding down
the back face of midocean swells.

A telescope reveals a nursery of LOLs
in the Milky Way's chaotic heart.

The body has a dream name and a metabolism
conserving energy in response to conditions.

Too soon the sun has horns that mirror
the horns teething from my head.

An unschooled survival instinct

A handwritten goodbye
crumples into underbelly softness
in your pocket.

We scrounge for birdsong
to keep you alive this week
and plot the city's free meals.

The lake's script is unreadable.
My love is a film projected
from an unknown distance
penetrating to such-and-such a depth.
Empathy playing out inaccuracies.
Knowing tensioned with not knowing.

Simply we have a safety plan and a connection
that arcs cryptically into our physical futures.
We count on robins and sparrows
and the candy-green co-starring leaves
not to use a dismissive tone,
not to shut us out.

Do no harm.
Do no harm.
Do no harm.
Do no harm.
Do no harm.
Do no harm.
Do no harm.
Do no harm.
Do no harm.
Do no harm.
Do no harm.
Do no harm.
Do no harm.
Do no harm.
Do no harm.
Do no harm.
Do no harm.
Do no harm.
Do no harm.
Do no harm.
Do no harm.
Do no harm.
Do no harm.
Do no harm.
Do no harm.
Do no harm.
Do no harm.
Do no harm.

Do no harm.
Do no harm.
Do no harm.
Do no harm.
Do no harm.
Do no harm.
Do no harm.
Do no harm.
Do no harm.

Wherein emptiness licks my lips.

Wherein emptiness is dehydrated and pees a deep yellow.

Wherein emptiness has a chest aging with sun.

Wherein emptiness presses the gas pedal.

Do no harm.
Do no harm.
Do no harm.
Do no harm.
Do no harm.
Do no harm.
Do no harm.
Do no harm.
Do no harm.
Do no harm.

Lake presents a felt condition

The drama of invertebrates and boggling
human behaviour, invariably married in a thriller,
clever and disturbing.

Lake holds space with the shoulders of a famous conductor
getting lost while stalking a moose, rationing cigarettes,
advocating a messy process.

A horizonless hour can be anchored
by back-channel willows, finely toothed,
aspirin leaves and bark.

Real remorse is a real achievement.
Self-compassion is a microleaf orienting
cell by cell to the sun.

I learn the same old things over and over.
The body has an ability to be reorganized crucially by contact.

Sometimes awareness like a seal comes searching,
pushing upriver from the sea, motion blur

      in muscular pulses,
           suddenly midlake

    a flash

    radiating from that head,
      low, swivelling.

More than the odd existential crisis in the mirror

Vulnerable, as we all are, to certain messaging,
contaminants pour through the channels.

Weather blows in without explanation for the fury.
A creature has slipped a glass case.

Clouds flow, drawn by wind
into the finest underfur.

Swooping across the uneasy air codes
in swallows' beaks, mud is transported.

A lake can't shake its sky awareness.
It flaunts an acquired ability to take it.

Tremendously electric,
not just a lot of whiskers,

lake aspires to build a reputation as a serious
documentarian contacting a present moment,

inviting feelings previously too dangerous
to feel, memories laid down before words.

No matter the dynamic range

There's a horizon we can't see beyond.

One bee visits my chest on repeat
freestyling through my ultraviolet
at deft angles. I feel annointed
and worried my jacket is its flower.

Infinity neverminding the guardrails,
        is that what stings
                (partly at least)
    in my wrong carrying,
        in my grasping
            wrongly an image
        to carry and carrying
                it wrongly.

The wrong windshield spidered
        and a forehead
            bleeding specifically.

The wrong malt breath
        above a child's face.

The wrong objects skittering
        on a shelf when.

Then unmoored

Obliged it seems to repeat
trauma as current experience.

Bathing every morning in pain's pulse,
      its twinge of arrogance,
            its nothing-but-this.

Another weapons builder labours at a lathe.
Another worker dies overheated in the sugar hold.
I want my oath of employment
to acknowledge the exposed lake beds,
the unprecedented flooding,
our nervous systems.

Pain cuts me into its signature move.

The cry I never forget reproduced
in a ditch, identifiably animal.

I can't word this.

Then do so poorly.

                  I remember
         having the legs of a foal and wanting
            to kick because there was air

The pain does not respond to logic

One ankle hangs off the end of the bed.
I don't want to look in the mirror ever again.

Doctors say there is a neural switch
common as dirt,
a regimen of daylight,
trying to sleep is not the way to woo sleep.

I can almost hear the slowly rebounding
tundra as the ice lifts, Celan's wheel
eating into the turf or is it
the grocery store freezers
keeping the popsicles and carcasses.

Age ten or so, I punched my best friend
in the gut over something that was nothing,
evidence of a single sequin of anger turned outward.

I can't access the rest.

                    stress dreams
                    derealization
                    free-floating
                    nerve pain
                    collage
                        of nonspecific symptoms
                        teetering
                            flint strike
                                amping inside

Biological needs dolphining
outside the range of known terrain,

my body wired like a troop of sailors
protecting their eyes from an ungodly reflectance.

Once I registered [   ] undreaming the blows.

I watched [   ] recalibrate night vision goggles.

[   ] spied their own lakehood
in the post-400-parts-per-million era.

Even water and air metabolize
violence
                    to a degree.

Now a hunch materializes—   Do something.
[   ] walks the sea's scrappy silks,   Do something.
in precious shoes, feet numb, the cold's   Do something.
ornamental daggers hopefully otherworldly   Do something.
enough to get through this night.   Do something.
                                                     Do something.
                                                     Do something.
                                                     Do something.
                                                     Do something.
                                                     Do something.
                                                     Do something.
                                                     Do something.
                                                     Do something.
                                                     Do something.
                                                     Do something.

Clouds consecrate any old suffering

Fluent in acceptance, the long view,
returning all children to their homes.
For each a lamb-cloud, well fed, frolicking,
fuzzball nosing your face skyward
and sorrowing your rain coast.

Between the high-rises, mosses
stash the clouds' offering.
Another color I can't describe arrives
        on or in the rivulets
so I message my impromptu therapist, a wren
re-hitching this to that so I might know a feeling.

I miss the dirty face, the bent knees,
the instinct that made fires.
The body on earth continues to eat,
conceivably poisoned, putting on a heavy coat
like caulking to stop up leaks,
heading out to return a swimsuit
or at least avoid talking.

> there I tend flurries of dust that might
>   knot into something
>   doubt is a turbulence
>   that could slide matter
>   into a hot core

> or dust could remain dust

All this description cannot be trusted

You know that, right?

The speed is wrong.

The wind inside the speed is missing.

The signal-to-noise ratio punishes our instruments.

Though we wave them anyway.

The wave itself now under puzzlement.

As motion being motion draws the eye.

Motion within the instrument's capacity.

Maybe motion just beyond.

Each instant overflows

Inch into the zapping cold
then plunge into
time's tearing chest sensation
mammalian diving reflex
a pulse that booms
then slows
glittering lashes blinking softly
elegant bubbles in slow-motion
ascent
smooth rotations
having nothing to do with effort
subject
of turbulence
minnows and other unregistered
cool-headed medics
press
to our human conducting
materials
alert
as hyphae lacing
minerals to the hemlocks
as water
rolling to the crowns
the lake
and its accomplices
latticing metabolism
taboo-green sourcing blue-heavens
polished into

a mysterious intercom
as pollen pulses
nutrients in
the body's spirited chemistry
hovering
near the pirouetting child
and the zooplankton's eye-pits
and the water molecules'
ultrasonic
attunement.

Ice lifts a paw, stealths a selfhood.
An unearthly hour chosen.
Rules not explained to the aspirant.
Only movement can know movement.

WATER TAKES UP THE OFFICE

In *Slouching Towards Bethlehem* (2000), the psychoanalyst Nina Coltart borrowed the term "bare attention," the common English translation of the Buddhist word *sati*, to describe the vital element in the therapeutic relationship. I find bare attention suggests simplicity and spareness, a fluency in following, in unknowing, free from conclusions and preconceived destinations, while at the same time embodying such alertness and flow.

Research shows that accurate empathy is the therapeutic ingredient that most consistently predicts positive change, no matter what the therapist's theoretical orientation. Given our own wounds, biases and mortal limits, bare attention must aim for a reflective element while remembering the imperfections inherent in any reflection.

In my experience, so much of empathy happens in wordless dimensions. As mammals we are able to register and tune in to a sophisticated symphony of signals, adapting and transforming in a reciprocal dance, creating together a dynamic system, similar to a lake, whose true shape is difficult or impossible to articulate.

OPEN-ENDED QUESTIONS SEEK THE REVELATION OF
SOCIAL CIRCUMSTANCES AND EMOTIONAL REACTIONS

This title is taken from the DSM-5 Pediatric Diagnostic Interview.

INTUITING SURVIVAL'S LIMNOLOGY

My practice is influenced by the ideas of response-based practice as articulated by Linda Coates, Cathy Richardson, Nick Todd and Allan Wade. Things that are often labelled as symptoms of psychological disorders—even the desire to die—can be seen and honoured as a valid protest against systemic, cultural conditions that are harmful.

This poem is informed by interpersonal neuroscience as communicated by Bruce Perry, Stephen Porges, Daniel Siegel, Bessel van der Kolk and others. While so much is still unknown, research in this field has offered helpful models for understanding how experiences of connection and disconnection shape us.

For so many people, violence, deprivation and neglect are daily experiences, and this sense of threat lives on in the body in myriad ways. Our medical and social support systems are incredibly inadequate, under-resourced and often perpetuate harm. While some therapies tend to pathologize individuals, I believe that therapy can name systems of oppression, honour the body's intelligences and protections and support the search for collective care, meaning making and flourishing.

I am indebted to the work of Val Plumwood. Her observation that "the hyper-separation and devaluation of the body and matter are not confined to ancient philosophy but are widespread in Western culture and were inherited by the dominant Western religious movements of Christianity" (*Controversies in Environmental Sociology*, 2004) resonates with my experience. Reclaiming a vibrant and sustainable relationship with our bodies can be part of creating a vibrant and sustainable relationship with the earth.

In the *Voronezh Notebooks*, written between 1935 and 1937, Osip Mandelstam argues that when we speak to each other, even with a simple word such as "sun," we are often so dull and desensitized that language can't ignite a connection, yet there exists a potential way to use words—for Mandelstam this is poetry—that "shakes us awake" and reveals an immense journey. Osip Mandelstam was exiled and died for his words in the Soviet labour camps shortly after my ancestors escaped that country.

This poem is inspired by Alice Oswald's translation of the *Iliad*'s "atmosphere" in *Memorial* (2011). I admire how her renditions of the soldiers' biographies achieve the "bright unbearable reality" of facing death.

The portraits in *Signal Infinities* are entirely fictional, though I aimed for an emotional resonance that pays homage to the vulnerability, dignity and truth-telling of those who have shared their stories with me. While maintaining strict confidentiality, I have tried to ask the lake to translate the energetic fields that have flowed over and around and through me.

The small catalogue on page 78 lists the names of people who have publicly told their stories of living through trauma and oppression that at times felt unliveable. Their stories can be found on the following websites:

Livethroughthis.org

Nowmattersnow.org

Wemattercampaign.org

988lifeline.org

White-nose syndrome, a fungal disease endangering bats, is driving bats to hibernate alone instead of in groups. Somehow, they seem to know something mysterious and deadly can pass between them.

Almost everything I know about moss is thanks to Robin Wall Kimmerer's book *Gathering Moss: A Natural and Cultural History of Mosses* (2003).

Stand.earth, an environmental organization, runs the Forest Eye website which uses government data, remote sensing and satellite imagery to document logging and road building in old growth forests in BC.

EVENTUALLY I ACKNOWLEDGE I CAN'T REALLY REMEMBER MY CHILDHOOD

The details of my ancestors' lives come from the writings of Abe Siebert, my grandfather, Cornelia Siebert (Neufeld), my grandmother, Gerhard Neufeld, my great grandfather, Johann Huebert, my great grandfather and Katharina Huebert (Siemens), my great grandmother. I am grateful to them for expressing and preserving the particulars of their joys and struggles. I aspire to their ways of peace, humility, service, devotion and integrity. And I continue to seek freedom from the shame and oppression that is a part of our heritage and to continue to awaken to a more enlivening relationship to all embodied presences.

Many thanks to Jeff Ganohalidoh Corntassel, citizen of the Cherokee Nation, who has shared some of the words that Indigenous peoples have used to describe settlers. In *Unsettling Settler Colonialism* (Snelgrove, Dhamoon, Corntassel, 2014), he says "Yonega is a Tsalagi (Cherokee) term for white settlers, which connotes 'foam of the water; moved by wind and without its own direction; clings to everything that's solid.' Wasicu is a Dakota term for settlers, which means 'takers of fat.' In the northwest, Hwunitum is a Hul'qumi'num and SENĆOŦEN word for settler, that some have described as 'the hungry people.'" When he spoke to a class I was in, he addressed those of us who are settlers and said, "These are the names you have been given. If you want a different name, you must earn it."

My gratitude to Pacheedaht Elder Bill Jones for his impassioned, eloquent spiritual and political guidance offered to the Ada'itsx / Fairy Creek movement to save the last fragments of ancient forests. And for allowing me to call on his words here.

This poem is dedicated to my best friend from those years. And to my parents—for the love you've lived and the grief you've held.

LAKE PRESENTS A FELT CONDITION

The description of the famous conductor was inspired by Lee Henderson's account of John Cage visiting Emma Lake in the article

"The Legacy of Saskatchewan's Most Controversial—and Impactful—Artist Program" published in *The Walrus* (Sep/Oct 2023).

CLOUDS CONSECRATE ANY OLD SUFFERING

I am influenced by the thinking of Emmanuel Levinas who was introduced to me through the teaching and writing of Mehmoona Moosa-Mitha. Though there are gaps and problems with Levinas's integration of his own ideas into his politics, I am nonetheless taken with his idea that ethics begins with an experience of another's infinity—of their innumerable circumstances and contingencies, their unknowable interiority, their beautiful strangeness, their ever becoming.

EACH INSTANT OVERFLOWS

"Only movement can know movement" is a line from Herakleitos.

Acknowledgements

I respectfully acknowledge the W̱SÁNEĆ Nations and the lək̓ ʷəŋən Peoples of the Songhees Nation and Esquimalt Nation whose relationships with their lands and waters shape their language, laws, political thought, ceremonies and creativity. I am grateful to the Elders and Knowledge Keepers who have welcomed me to their homelands. I aim to live up to the responsibilities of this welcome.

For sharing difficult and vital stories and wisdom, deepest thanks to: STOL₵EȽ John Elliot (W̱JOȽEȽP/Tsartlip Nation), Elder Sellemah Joan Morris (Songhees Nation) and Elder Bill Jones (Pacheedaht Nation).

Thank you to Nick XEMŦOLTW̱ Claxton for teachings in Indigenous resurgence, alongside W̱SÁNEĆ carver Perry LaFortune who through teaching us to carve a canoe and paddles also taught deep listening to trees and to one another.

I am so grateful to SȾÁ,UTW̱ (Tsawout Nation) Elders Vic and Joyce Underwood for sharing their cultural teachings and ceremonies and for helping me learn to speak from the heart.

For dedicated work in land and cultural revitalization and welcoming settlers to learn and lend a hand, thanks to: Cheryl Bryce, Knowledge Keeper and force behind the Lekwungen Community Toolshed, Sarah Jim, land steward with PEPÁḴEN HÁUTW̱ and the leading light of the W̱SÍ,ḴEM Ivy Project (Healing the Place of Clay) and Tiffany Joseph, inspiring coordinator of the Rematriate Stewardship project with the XAXE TEṈEW̱ Sacred Land Society. The physical act of joining with others to help heal and protect the land has been so healing to me in return.

I lift my hands to all the land defenders and water keepers.

Thank you to my teachers: Cathy Richardson (Métis) and Allan Wade, for the dignity and elegance in response-based practice; Susan Strega, for a social justice approach to collaborative conversations;

Donna Jeffery, for never-ending critical reflections on whiteness and the desire to be good; Yvonne Haist, for the integration of trauma theory, interpersonal neurobiology and social justice; Jennifer White, for critical suicidology; Renee Linklater (Rainy River First Nations), for thinking and writing on decolonizing trauma work; Vikki Reynolds, for the active ideas of justice-doing, resisting burn-out and naming the spiritual pain involved in this work; Todd Ormiston (Northern Tutchone/Tlingit), for bringing laughter and ceremony into decolonizing policy and practice; David Segal and Katy Rose, for such creativity and leadership in nature-based therapy.

Special thanks to Mehmoona Moosa-Mitha, whose stirring class on feminist, anti-oppressive and Levinasian ethics was the initial spark for this poem.

Thank you to my colleagues at Foundry and on the High Risk Team at Child and Youth Mental Health—I learned so much from each one of you. I have such gratitude for my clinical supervisors and consul-tants who navigated many difficult dilemmas with me: Cheryl Turner, Lori McKeown, Kathy Campos, Iris Elsdon, Kirsteen Moore, Amanda Turner and Caylee Villette. Extra special thanks to Stacy Folk—you have the capacity to see into the deep and have shored me up.

I have been changed by the good work of Corinne Diachuk, Julie Giroux, Ocean Lum, Jude Marleau, Liam 'Captain' Snowdon and Anna Stein. Immense gratitude to my therapist Lisa Mortimore who helped me feel and believe the knowing of my body and explore the field beyond good and bad.

Thank you to my dream team of embodied healers: Bryn Thompson, Ange Vander Schilden and Meg Aris. You have truly moved and breathed with me through pain, shame and vulnerability towards new freedoms.

Utmost gratitude to all the plants and animals who too have shone their infinity my way. You have taught me the wonders of sunning, stretching, moving, touching, eating and just being a body among bodies. And to the lakes and rivers, my beloved water bodies.

Am I able to be thankful to pain and disability? That's something I can't quite say.

Thank you to the stellar team at McClelland & Stewart. Chimedum Ohaegbu, Peter Norman, Dylan Browne, Sean Tai and Ruta Liormonas—thank you for contributing your talents to this book. Immense gratitude to Canisia Lubrin for your poetic vision and heart. And to Kelly Joseph for shepherding every big and little thing so gracefully.

I am honoured that Christina Mackie lent her moving painting of the deep to this work.

The writing of *Signal Infinities* was supported by the Canada Council for the Arts and the BC Arts Council. The Writers' Trust 5 x 5 Award was a great boost at a time of no sure thing—thank you to Esi Edugyan for believing in my work. I am grateful for residencies at the Banff Centre for the Arts, the Pierre Berton House and the Sointula Art Shed and for the lively community of artists in each place.

For editorial guidance in the very early stages of this work, heartfelt thanks to Karen Solie and Jan Zwicky.

Thank you to Emily Nilsen and Sara Cassidy for providing helpful feedback on the manuscript.

Lorna Crozier, Patrick Lane and Tim Lilburn made me believe in poetry as a way of life. Ali Blythe, Garth Martens and Anne-Marie Turza make a poetic fire that warms me to the core.

Deepest thanks to Anne-Marie for ingenious editorial insights. Your integration of poetics, ethics and whimsy is my Polaris.

Ali, my stedfast one, for all you do and are. You read my every word, my every move with such attention, intelligence and care.

Thank you to my family and ancestors for so much love. Never-ending gratitude to my parents, Phil and Shirl Siebert, for a home full of words and music, and countless adventures beyond.

Signal Infinities is dedicated to every person who has explored with me what makes life worth living.

And to all the healers and artists tending pain, tending dignity, practicing presence.

MELANIE SIEBERT is the author of *Deepwater Vee*, a finalist for the Governor General's Literary Award for Poetry. Her nonfiction book *Heads Up: Changing Minds on Mental Health* won the Lane Anderson Award for best science writing for young readers in Canada and was a finalist for the Sheila A. Egoff Children's Literature Prize. Melanie grew up in Treaty 6 territory in Saskatchewan, raised as a white, third-generation settler of European/Mennonite heritage. She now lives in the Pacific Northwest on the beautiful homelands of the W̱SÁNEĆ Nations and the lək̓ʷəŋən Peoples of the Songhees and Esquimalt Nations. Melanie practices attachment-focused and nature-based therapy in Victoria, BC.